# WISHING on a STAR

## Constellation Stories and Stargazing Activities for Kids

## FRAN LEE

GIBBS·SMITH
P
PUBLISHER

Salt Lake City

For Ted, Travis (and Scooter!),
and for Joey, my kitty-cat constellation.

With thanks to
Madge Baird, Suzanne Taylor, and Monica Weeks.

—FL

★ ★ ★

First Edition

01 02 03 04 05    5 4 3 2 1

Text and illustrations copyright © 2001 by Fran Lee

This is a Gibbs Smith Junior book, published by
Gibbs Smith, Publisher
P.O. Box 667
Layton, Utah 84041

To order: (1-800) 748-5439
www.gibbs-smith.com

Edited by Monica Weeks
Designed by Fran Lee
Printed and bound in Hong Kong

NOTE: Some of the activities suggested in this book require adult assistance and supervision, as noted throughout. The publisher and author assume no responsibility for any damages or injuries incurred while performing any of the activities in this book.

**Library of Congress Cataloging-in-Publication Data**

Lee, Fran.
    Wishing on a star : constellation stories and stargazing activities for kids / written and illustrated by Fran Lee.
        p. cm.
    ISBN 1-58685-029-6
        1. Constellations—Juvenile literature. 2. Constellations—Observers' manuals—Juvenile literature. [1. Constellations. 2. Constellations—Folklore.] I. Title.

QB63 .L38 2001
523.8—dc21

00-045002

# Contents

# About the Activities

Ask a grown-up to help you with these activities so they'll be safe and fun!

If your glow-in-the-dark paint loses its oomph, RECHARGE it by shining a flashlight at it.

## PATTERN TRANSFER METHOD

You'll need to make the patterns in this book bigger and copy them onto other paper before starting most of these projects. A copy machine or a computer with a scanner and a printer will make this job easy.

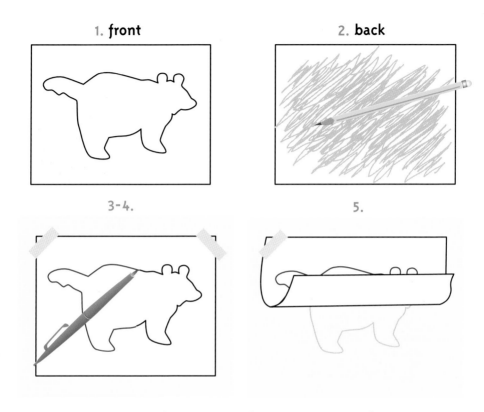

**1. front**

**2. back**

**3-4.**

**5.**

## Follow these steps for a smooth pattern transfer:

1. Copy the pattern from the book onto copy paper. A grown-up assistant can help you make it the right size! *(Adults, enlarge your copy to the percentage noted next to the pattern.)*

2. On the back of your copy-paper pattern, rub a pencil back and forth, making sure the lead covers where the picture is on front.

3. Place your copy pattern (penciled side down) on the surface that you want to paint or cut out. Tape the copy paper lightly in position.

4. With a ballpoint pen, trace the pattern outline. Press a little harder than you usually do. Be sure to go over every line carefully.

5. To see the pattern on the new surface, lift the tape off the paper carefully, one piece at a time.

*See the pattern transferred onto the surface?*

# Introduction

**"When you wish upon a star, your dreams come true."**
*Jiminy Cricket*

If you go outside on a clear night, you can't help yourself. Your head tilts back, your eyes rise up, and you find yourself gazing at the stars in the dark sky . . . WOW! From the very beginning of time, people all over the world have cherished the night sky's amazing beauty and mystery.

How old are the stars? They're older than you and me, older than our parents, and even older than our grandmas and grandpas. In fact, they're older than the oldest thing you can think of! Some stars are more than billions of years old, and some more than billions of miles away! When you look at the stars, it's like looking back in time.

Did you know that the patterns and shapes made by these bright stars tell stories? In fact, the night sky is our oldest picture book. Ancient people—including Native Americans, Chinese, Romans, Greeks, Indians,

and Babylonians—identified groups of stars called *constellations* (pro-nounced kahn-stell-AY-shuns) and made up stories about them. We call these stories *legends*.

The most famous constellation legends came from the Greeks and Egyptians. There were 48 constellations identified during ancient times by the Greek astronomer Ptolemy (tall-uh-MEE). These constellations were believed to represent figures of heroes and heroines, animals and creatures, and unusual objects. Their stories can be magical, beautiful, ugly, scary, romantic, mysterious, or amazing—but they are always exciting!

In this book we will explore the star maps and legends of nine fascinat-ing constellations. Fun activities and projects will help us celebrate the stars.

So, go outside, and tilt your head back . . . WOW!

# Ursa Major & Ursa Minor
## The Big Bear & the Little Bear

Ursa Major is a constellation in the shape of a big bear, so it is sometimes called the Big Bear. Right above Ursa Major is Ursa Minor, or the Little Bear. Do you see something unusual about these bears? Their tails seem to be longer than your average bear's! The ancient Greeks have a tale for how these long tails came to be.

Zeus (ZOOS) was the king of all the gods in the heavens. He led a very exciting life, traveling between the earth and the heavens. One day, as Zeus was walking through a wooded area on earth, he came upon the young huntress Callisto (kuh-LIS-toe). He thought she was very beautiful. Zeus's wife, Hera (HARE-uh), was jealous, so she used her goddess powers to turn Callisto into a big bear.

As a bear, Callisto had a hard life. She missed her son Arcus (AHR-cus). In addition, the friends she used to hunt with now hunted her. One day, while young Arcus was hunting, he aimed his arrow at Callisto, not realizing that the bear was his mother. Luckily, Zeus was passing by at that moment and jumped between Arcus and Callisto. Zeus told Arcus to put his bow down, then changed him into a little bear. To keep mother and son together and out of harm's way, Zeus threw the two bears into the night sky. They became the constellations Ursa Major and Ursa Minor, or, as we like to call them, the Big Bear and the Little Bear.

How did those bears get long tails? According to legend, the mighty Zeus stretched their tails as he tossed them into the night sky.

The bears' tails form the handles of the Big Dipper and the Little Dipper, which are the famous star patterns inside Ursa Major and Ursa Minor. A star pattern within a larger constellation is called an *asterism*. The Big Dipper is the easiest of all asterisms to see because its stars shine brighter than almost all the others.

At the tip of Ursa Minor's tail (or the Little Dipper's handle) is the star called Polaris (poh-LARE-us), or the North Star.

# How to Find the Big Dipper & the Little Dipper (and Ursa Major & Ursa Minor)

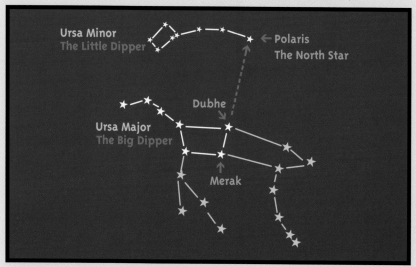

The Big Dipper is easiest to find in the spring, when it is right over our heads in the Northern Hemisphere. The farther north you are, the clearer and brighter the Big Dipper becomes. To find it, look for a giant teacup or saucepan with a curved handle. Within the constellation Ursa Major, the Big Dipper forms the tail and back part of the bear's body. Can you find the rest of the bear?

There are seven main stars in the Big Dipper. The stars Merak (MƐƐ-rak) and Dubhe (DOO-bee) at the far edges of the cup point in a straight line towards the North Star. The North Star is the last star in the tail of the Little Dipper, the asterism in Ursa Minor.

When you face the North Star, you are facing north. East is to your right, west is to your left, and south is behind you. Polaris is visible from everywhere on earth. It is the guiding light for world travelers.

# Big Dipper Glow-in-the-Dark Star Map

Big Dipper Star Pattern    200%

Make a Glow-in-the-Dark Star Map of the Big Dipper. Then head outside on a clear night and see if you can match up your glowing map with the real thing.

1. Paint the white construction paper with glow-in-the-dark paint, covering the entire paper. Let it dry.

2. Using the Big Dipper Star Pattern and the Pattern Transfer Method on pages 2 and 3, draw seven stars on the glow-in-the-dark paper with a pencil.

3. Cut out the seven stars.

4. Follow the Big Dipper Star Pattern and glue the stars onto the black construction paper. Use a white pencil or chalk to connect the stars.

5. Make a label for your map that says The Big Dipper.

You can make Glow-in-the-Dark Star Maps for all of your favorite constellations and asterisms.

## Materials

Black construction paper (8 ½ x 11 inches)
White construction paper (8 ½ x 11 inches)
White glue
Tape
Scissors
Pencil and pen
Glow-in-the-dark paint
Paintbrush
White pencil or chalk
Big Dipper Star Pattern

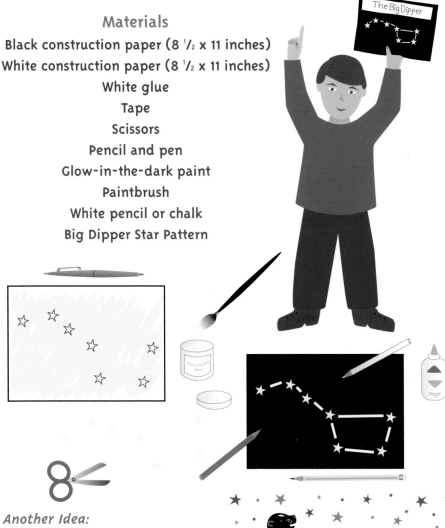

*Another Idea:*

Put a star map on the ceiling or wall of your bedroom (with permission from a parent, of course). Make as many glow-in-the-dark stars as you will need. Tape them (don't use glue here!) to your ceiling or wall in the pattern of your favorite constellation or asterism.

Cool!

Among the twinkles, can you see that the stars are different colors? The coolest stars are red, and the hottest ones are blue.

# Leo Major
## The Great Lion

I n the constellation Leo (LEE-oh), the Great Lion's mane can be found by looking for a backward question mark in the sky. The ancient astronomers called this a sickle (a tool used for harvesting wheat). They said that when the sun entered Leo, summer would begin.

Early Egyptians and Babylonians tell the story of Physbe (FIZ-bee) and Peranese (PARE-uh-NEES). Physbe and Peranese were in love, but their parents would not let them see each other. So they found a secret hiding place in the forest, near a pond. One night while Physbe was waiting for Peranese to join her at the pond, a lion came along to enjoy a drink of water with his supper. Physbe went running through the woods to warn Peranese about the lion, losing her veil along the way. Little did she know that Peranese was almost to the pond, and he was shocked by what he saw when he got there. There was no sign of Physbe, only her veil in the middle of the lion's supper!

Well, you can imagine what Peranese thought. He was so sad that he felt he could never be happy again. He took his sword and shoved it through his heart. When Physbe found him dead, she used that same sword on herself. The Babylonian gods placed the lion and Physbe's veil in the night sky as a reminder to all of this sad tale.

## How To Find Leo Major

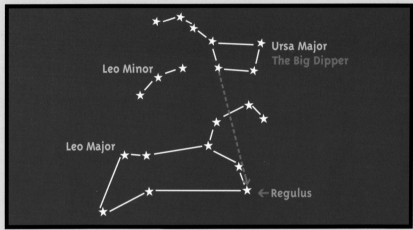

Leo can be found just below the cup of the Big Dipper in Ursa Major. Look for the two stars of the cup next to the handle. Draw a straight line down to find Regulus (reh-GYOO-lus), the brightest star in Leo.

The star Regulus (the point at the bottom of the question mark) is also called the Lion's Heart.

In the ancient Greek legend, the Great Lion lived on the moon and came to earth riding on a falling star.

# Leo the Lion Glow-in-the-Dark Mobile

If you hang this mobile in your room, you will see Leo Major dancing with the stars at night before you close your eyes and go to sleep.

## Materials

Newspaper

Wire or plastic clothes hanger

1 spool of yarn or ribbon

1 spool of string

1 sheet of cardboard (8 ½ x 11 inches)

2 sheets white construction paper (8 ½ x 11 inches)

Scissors

Pencils and pen

Hole punch

White glue

Paintbrush

Glow-in-the-dark paint

Black tempera paint

Leo the Lion Pattern (p. 16)

Leo Star Pattern (p. 17)

Leo Parts Pattern (p. 18)

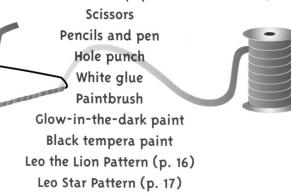

Leo the Lion Pattern      200%

1. Cover your worktable with newspaper to protect it from any spills.

2. Wrap your hanger with your favorite color of yarn or ribbon. Glue or tie it at the ends.

3. Trace the Leo the Lion Pattern onto the cardboard, using the Pattern Transfer Method on pages 2 and 3. Cut out the shape.

4. Paint both sides of the cardboard lion with black tempera paint. Let the first side dry before painting the other side, then let that side dry.

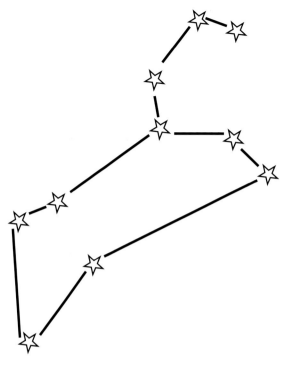

Leo Star Pattern     200%

5. Punch two holes in the lion, marked with Xs on the pattern.

6. Paint the two sheets of white construction paper with glow-in-the-dark paint. Let dry.

7. Using the Pattern Transfer Method, trace the Leo Star Pattern onto one sheet of the painted construction paper. Cut out the stars. (Save the leftover paper—you'll need it later!)

8. Glue these stars (glow side up) onto one side of Leo. Follow the Leo Star Map for placement.

9. From the second sheet of construction paper, use the Pattern Transfer Method and Leo Parts Pattern to trace and cut out the lion's ear, whiskers, nose, mouth, mane, toenails, and tuft of tail. Glue these (glow side up) to the other side of the lion.

10. Cut one 7-inch piece of string. Tie one end to the hole in the lion's back. Tie the other end to the bottom of the hanger. You can adjust the lengths of your pieces of string to achieve the perfect balance.

Leo Parts Pattern    200%

11. Cut one 4-inch piece of string. Tie one end to the hole in the lion's head. Tie the other end to the bottom of the hanger. Adjust the string and balance so Leo hangs like a sign from your hanger.

12. Cut two large glow-in-the-dark stars out of leftover construction paper. Punch a hole at the top of each. Cut two pieces of string for the stars. The strings can be as long as you want. Tie these stars with string and hang them on either side of Leo. These stars represent Physbe and Peranese.

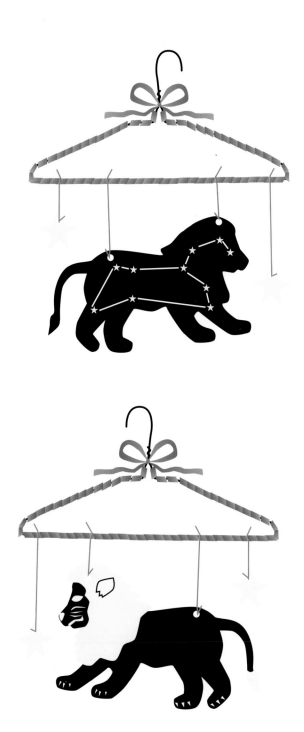

# Orion
## The Great Hunter

According to Greek mythology, Orion (oh-RYE-un) was the biggest, strongest, and most handsome man in the world. He was also the best hunter. In the constellation Orion, the hunter carries a shield in his left hand, a club in his right, and a sword in his belt.

The Greek legend follows Orion on his many adventures, including a period of blindness. After Orion was struck blind, he went in search of a cure for his blindness. A Cyclops (SIGH-clops), a giant man with one eye in the middle of his forehead, guided him to the sun god Helios (HEE-lee-os). Orion asked Helios to give back his sight, and Helios granted Orion's wish. The sun's warm morning rays worked a miracle, and Orion could see again.

With his newfound vision, it was not long before Orion spotted the beautiful Artemis (are-tuh-mus). She was the goddess of the moon and a devoted huntress. Orion and Artemis became inseparable friends, hunting and roaming the woods together. But Artemis's brother, the god Apollo, did not like what he had heard about Orion. In jealous concern for his sister, Apollo ended Artemis's friendship with the great hunter. He tossed a deadly scorpion at Orion's feet and it stung him, causing him to die. Artemis was so saddened by the loss of her friend Orion that she placed him among the stars of the night sky where she could always see him.

In honor of the scorpion's defeat of Orion, the gods placed the scorpion in the heavens and named the constellation Scorpio (score-pee-oh).

# How to Find Orion

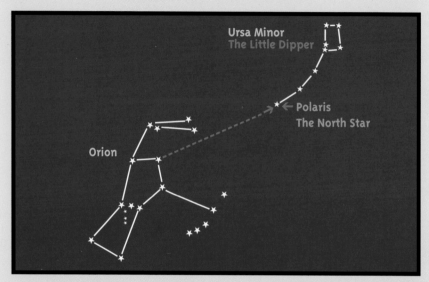

In North America, Orion can be seen directly overhead in the southern part of the sky during the autumn, winter, and spring. In the winter, it is the brightest constellation in the sky. The best times to see Orion are December through March. During summer, Orion follows too close to the sun to be seen at night.

Orion is easily found because the many bright stars that make up this constellation form an outline of the great hunter. His body is shaped like an hourglass, and a sword hangs from his belt. He holds a shield in his left hand and a raised club in his right. But the brightest stars in Orion are the three that make up his belt. These three stars are in a straight line. They are used to measure distance in this part of the sky. The star that represents Orion's head points to the North Star.

To keep Orion busy, the gods also put the constellation Taurus (TAHR-us), the charging bull, in the stars just out of his reach.

# Paper Bag Lantern / Star Maps

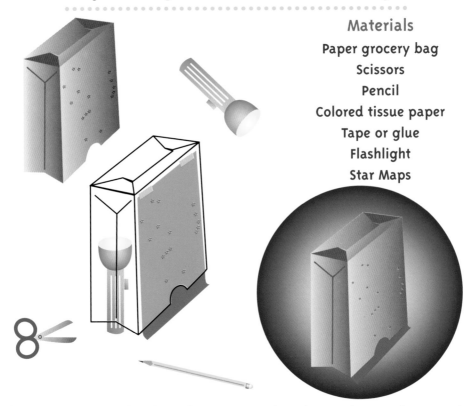

## Materials

Paper grocery bag
Scissors
Pencil
Colored tissue paper
Tape or glue
Flashlight
Star Maps

Think of the stars that have been our guides—the North Star, the Star of Bethlehem, even the Sun. Our bag lanterns, glowing with the star maps of Orion, Scorpio, and Taurus, will help guide us when we put them outside at night or in a dark room.

1. Use the Pattern Transfer Method described on pages 2 and 3 to trace these patterns onto the bag with a pencil.
2. Cut out the star shapes.
3. Glue or tape a piece of colored tissue paper inside the bag behind the cut-out shapes.
4. Stand a flashlight on the ground pointing up to the sky. Place the bag over it and see the stars glow!

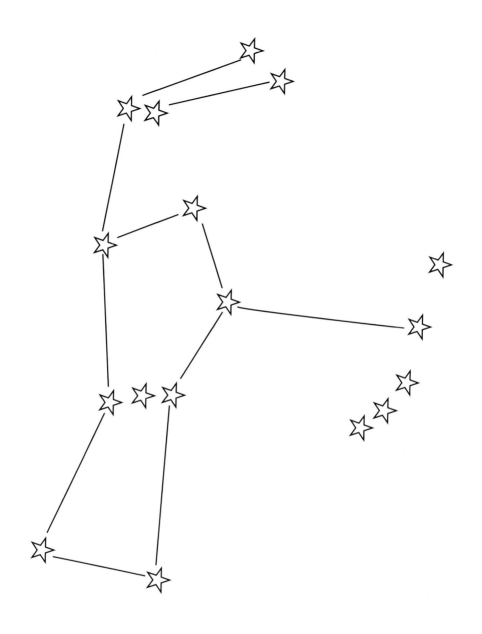

**Orion Star Pattern**     175%

For these star transfers, use 11 x 17-inch copy paper, or copy onto two sheets of 8 ½ x 11-inch paper and piece together with clear tape.

Scorpio Star Pattern
Once at 200% and again at 140%

Taurus Star Pattern
Once at 200% and again at 140%

On the other side of my bag,
I used my colored pencils to draw a picture
of Orion, the Great Hunter!

# Canis Major & Canis Minor

## The Great Dog & the Little Dog

A legend from India about Canis (KAY-nus) Major tells a story of a dog and five brothers who were princes. Bhima (buh-HEE-muh) was the happiest prince, Arjuna (AHR-joon) the strongest, Nakula (nah-KOO-luh) the best looking, Sahadeva (sah-hah-DAY-vuh) the wisest, and Yudistira (yoo-DISH-truh) the oldest. Yudistira's dog Svana (SFAHN-uh) rounded out the group. Traveling together, they left their home to seek the Kingdom of Heaven.

The first stop they made was at a country fair. There, people were singing, dancing, and having a party, and Bhima felt right at home. He decided to stay, saying to himself, "I will relax here, have fun, be happy. I will search for the Kingdom of Heaven tomorrow." So Yudistira, his dog

Svana, and his brothers Arjuna, Nakula, and Sahadeva wished Bhima well and left without him.

On the road, they came upon an army of soldiers lining up to face their enemy. Arjuna could only think of one thing: he must lead these men into battle. He said, "Today I will be strong for my country, and tomorrow I will find the Kingdom of Heaven." So Yudistira, his dog Svana, and his brothers Nakula and Sahadeva wished Arjuna well and went on without him.

After traveling all night, they stopped to rest at the edge of a beautiful garden with waterfalls and flowers of every color. There was also a pretty little princess walking in the garden. When the princess and Nakula spotted each other, it was love at first sight. He said to himself, "I will stay here with this princess today, and tomorrow I will discover the Kingdom of Heaven." So Yudistira, his dog Svana, and his brother Sahadeva wished Nakula well and went on without him.

Next they reached a great university where Sahadeva found subjects he would like to study. He said to himself, "I will stay here today and grow wiser, and tomorrow I will look for the Kingdom of Heaven." So Yudistira and his dog Svana wished Sahadeva well and went on without him.

Finally, they climbed Mount Meru (MEE-ruh) and stood before the gates of heaven. Indra (IN-druh), Lord of Past and Present, invited Yudistira to enter the gates. "This is just what I came here to do," replied Yudistira, "but only if I may bring my dog Svana with me."

"I'm sorry," said Indra, "but heaven is no place for dogs. Leave this dog and follow me."

Hearing that, Yudistira turned away, saying, "If Svana can't go to heaven, then I will not go either."

"But you left your four brothers behind," answered Indra. "Why can't you leave this dog?"

"Indra, Lord of Past and Present," said Yudistira as he bowed his head, "I did not leave my brothers. They left me to follow their hearts' desires. I will not leave this dog Svana, for he has given his heart to me. I would rather not enter heaven if that means leaving him."

Indra was impressed with this answer and invited both Yudistira and Svana to enter paradise. He set the constellation Canis Major, the Great Dog, in the night sky to honor Yudistira and Svana's devotion to each other. Later, Canis Minor, the Little Dog, was added to keep the big dog company!

# How to Find Canis Major, Canis Minor, and Sirius

The best time to see Canis Major is on a clear night from January through March. Follow Orion's belt south to the next bright star, and you have found Sirius (SIR-ee-us), the Dog Star. Sirius is at the shoulder of the Great Dog and is the brightest star in the night sky.

Sirius rises during the hottest days of summer. The early Egyptians believed that the appearance of Sirius in the sky before sunrise marked the beginning of their growing season. At that time, the Nile River would overflow and bring new silt and water to the land, enriching, irrigating, and fertilizing the soil. Farmers called these days (from July to early September) the Dog Days.

The best time to see Canis Minor is December through May. It is located just north of Canis Major. Though Canis Minor is one of the smallest constellations (just two stars), one of its stars, Procyon (PRO-see-on), which has a yellowish-white glow, is also one of the brightest stars in the night sky. *Procyon* is a Greek word meaning "before the dog."

The word **canis** comes from the Latin word for "dog."

In the Greek myth, Canis Major and his companion Canis Minor were Orion's hunting dogs. To honor the dogs' speed and faithfulness, Zeus placed Canis Major and Canis Minor in the heavens.

# Constellation Picture Book

The constellation Canis Major tells a story about a faithful dog that was honored for his loyalty. Now you can make a picture book that tells a story about an imaginary constellation, honoring your favorite animal friend. It can be about a beloved pet or maybe even an animal found on a farm or in a zoo.

Create and draw the star map for your constellation. What is your constellation's name? Be sure to record the date, time, and place where you first "discovered" your constellation. Make colorful pictures about the important and heroic stories from your animal's life. You may also want to save some pages in your book for writing your animal friend's legend. Share your book with friends and family.

## Materials (for one book)

2 sheets of cardboard or chip board (8 ½ x 11 inches)
4 to 8 sheets of white construction paper (8 x 10 ½ inches)
Rubber band
Scissors
Hole punch
1 spool of ribbon or sturdy string
Colored pencils, markers, or crayons
White glue
Glitter
Paintbrushes
Glow-in-the-dark paint
Things to decorate your book
(stickers, dried flowers, leaves, magazine pictures, colored construction paper, etc.)
Newspaper

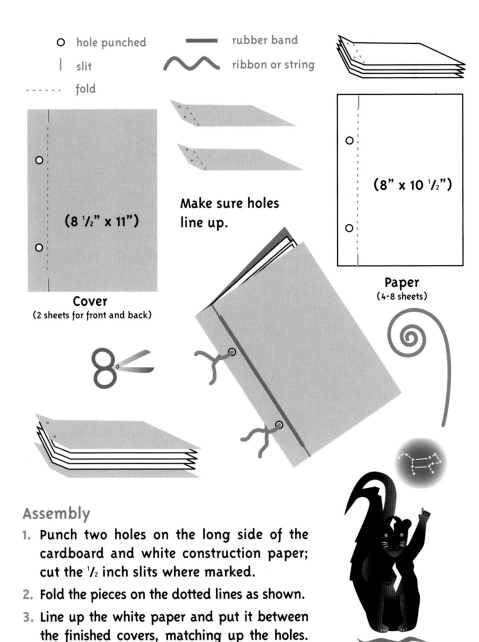

| o | hole punched | ▬▬▬ | rubber band |
| I | slit | ∿ | ribbon or string |
| - - - - - - | fold | | |

(8 ½" x 11")

**Cover**
(2 sheets for front and back)

Make sure holes line up.

(8" x 10 ½")

**Paper**
(4-8 sheets)

## Assembly

1. Punch two holes on the long side of the cardboard and white construction paper; cut the ½ inch slits where marked.

2. Fold the pieces on the dotted lines as shown.

3. Line up the white paper and put it between the finished covers, matching up the holes. Place a tight rubber band around the book, fitting it into the slits as shown. Tie pieces of ribbon or string through each of the holes.

Have you ever heard of the Great Skunk constellation?

## Design

1. Put your constellation's name on the cover of your book as its title. For this, you may want to find letters or words in magazines, or you can cut out letters from construction paper. You can also use markers and glow-in-the-dark paint to spell out the name.

2. On the cover, squeeze out the glue to form star shapes and pour the glitter over the glue. (Be careful not to overdo it with the glitter!) Dust the remaining glitter off and onto the newspaper. Let the glue dry. Decorate the front and back covers and the inside pages of your book using the materials you've gathered. Cut out colorful constellation shapes from the construction paper and paste them into the book. Cut out pictures and words from the magazines and paste them into the book.

3. Remember to put your name on the cover—after all, you are the author!

**P**rom Greek mythology comes the story of Pegasus (PEH-guh-sus), the
Winged Horse. Pegasus was born as a beautiful, fully grown horse with
wings. He was the son of Medusa (mih-DOO-suh), the famous Gorgon with
hair of snakes and skin of dragon-like scales, and Poseidon (pu-SIGH-dun),
the god of the sea. One day Prince Bellerophon (buh-LAIR-uh-fun) tried to
use Pegasus for his own selfish purposes. He ordered Pegasus to carry him
to Mount Olympus (uh-LIM-pus) to be made a god. Zeus was so shocked by
Bellerophon's rudeness that he pushed him off Pegasus, allowing only
Pegasus to fly to the gods. From that time forward, Pegasus flew between
the earth and the heavens, carrying Zeus's heavy thunderbolts.

# How to Find Pegasus

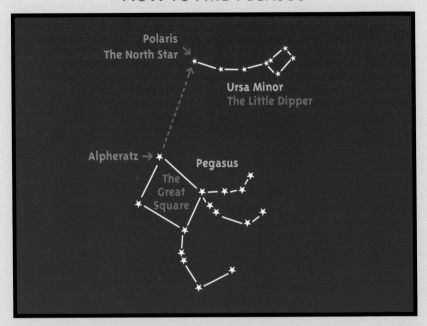

The best time of the year to find Pegasus is from August to October, when the winged horse appears upside down. Look for the asterism called The Great Square, formed by four bright stars. You can find The Great Square by tracing a straight line from the North Star towards the northeast. The North Star is lined up with two of the stars in the square. The Great Square is the easiest part of Pegasus to see. Some astronomers say that the square forms Pegasus's wings, and others say it forms the body of the horse.

The most famous star in the Pegasus constellation is called Alpheratz (alf-uh-ratz). It can be seen directly overhead at midnight on September 23, the first day of autumn. A star that is found directly overhead is called a **zenith** (ZEE-nuth) star. Alpheratz is the beginning point of all the constellations in the night sky, and used by astronomers and navigators to map the stars.

# Twinkling Pegasus Thaumatrope

What makes the stars twinkle?

Astronomers say that a star's light becomes a very bright beam by the time it enters Earth's atmosphere. Bouncing off particles in the air, the light beam splits into many beams and appears to twinkle. The scientific name for the twinkling of stars is *stellar scintillation* (stel-lar sin-tuh-LAY-shun). The word *stellar* means "of the stars."

I think a star twinkles because it is winking at us, saying hello!

Hi!

A thaumatrope (THAW-muh-TROHP) is a little card that has different pictures on opposite sides. When the card is twirled, the pictures appear to combine with each other. For example, when you spin a thaumatrope with a horse on one side and a cowboy on the other, you will see a cowboy riding a horse! This is a visual trick used in animation.

You can make a Pegasus thaumatrope by putting wings on one side of the card and a horse on the other.

## Materials

Pegasus Thaumatrope Pattern
Sturdy white paper
Black and red felt-tip markers
Scissors
Small hole punch
2 pieces of sturdy string or thin yarn, about 5 inches long

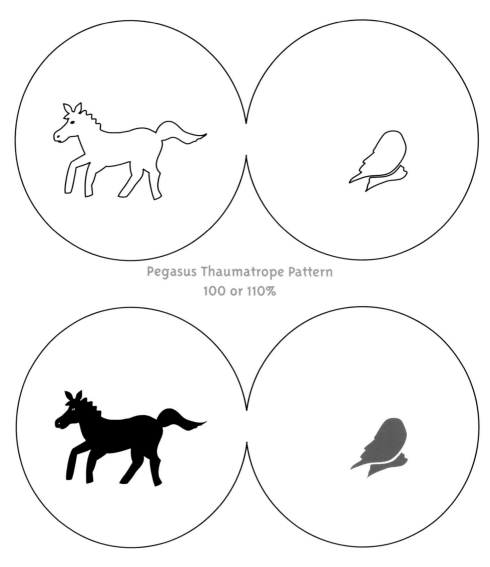

Pegasus Thaumatrope Pattern
100 or 110%

1. Copy the Pegasus Thaumatrope Pattern onto sturdy white paper and cut out. Color the wings with the red marker and the horse with the black marker.

2. Fold the circles together so the images are facing out on opposite sides.

3. Punch holes through both sides where marked (see page 39).

4. Tie and knot one end of each string through the two layers of each hole, with one string on each side.

5. Hold your thaumatrope by each string in either hand, and twist back and forth. Watch the wings and horse combine to make Pegasus twinkle!

# Coma Berenices

## Berenice's Hair

I n this ancient Greek legend, Berenice (bare-uh-nees) had the most beautiful hair. She wore it in one long shiny braid down her back. Her husband King Ptolemy (tall-uh-MEE) told her that he must leave their home and go on a dangerous mission to protect his land and people. "Oh, dear," Berenice said, "What can I do to make sure he returns safely?"

After thinking about it for a while, Berenice decided to cut off her lovely braid of hair and place it in the temple of Venus (VEE-nus), the goddess of love and beauty. This was her sacrifice to keep her husband safe.

When King Ptolemy arrived home unharmed, Berenice learned that her hair was missing from the temple. She became upset. However, Zeus had decided that Berenice's hair belonged in the night skies. This constellation would remind us of the sacrifice Berenice made for her husband. When Berenice found this out, she was quite satisfied.

# How to Find Coma Berenices

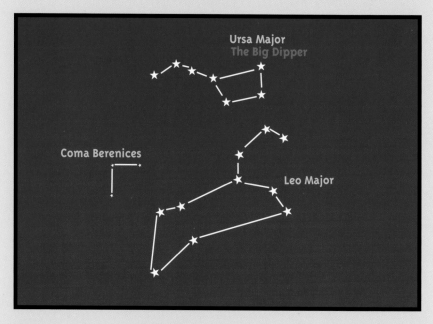

Ursa Major
The Big Dipper

Coma Berenices

Leo Major

The best time to find Coma Berenices is during spring and summer. It is a very old constellation, and it is so far away that it is also very dim and very small. Coma Berenices is one of the farthest constellations from the Milky Way. When you look for Coma Berenices, face north and look straight up. There you can see the whole galaxy and beyond. It is placed just above Leo's tail and just below the handle of the Big Dipper.

Find Leo, and look for the tuft at the end of his tail. This is Berenice's hair! These stars have also been called "The Tuft in Leo's Tail."

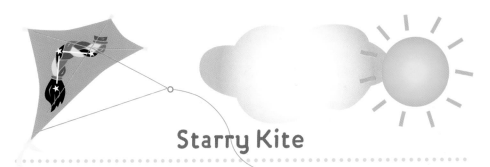

# Starry Kite

Make a starry kite to remember the beautiful Coma Berenices.

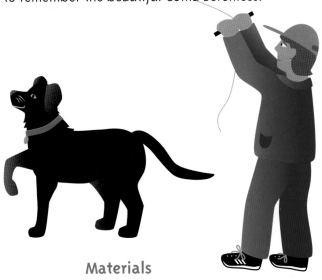

## Materials
Craft paper or heavy construction paper, 38 x 38 inches
2 dowels (square sections of hardwood or soft wood), 36 and 33 inches
Kite spool with string
Scissors
Small saw or knife to cut notch in wood *(Adult help required)*
Pencil
Glue
Tempera paint
Tape
Plastic towing ring
Lightweight cloth or tissue paper (enough for a tail)

43

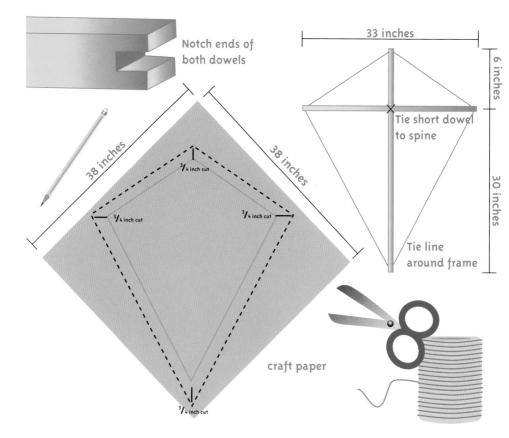

Notch ends of both dowels

33 inches

6 inches

Tie short dowel to spine

30 inches

38 inches

38 inches

³/₄ inch cut

³/₄ inch cut

³/₄ inch cut

³/₄ inch cut

Tie line around frame

craft paper

1. Cut notches in both ends of both dowels. Tie the short (cross) dowel to the longer (spine) dowel, as shown in the illustration. Then tie a piece of string around the frame, fitting it tightly into each of the notches.

2. Use the frame as a pattern for your kite by laying it flat on the craft paper and drawing a line around the frame. Cut the diamond shape out of the paper, leaving an extra ³/₄-inch hem around the edges so you can attach the kite to the frame.

3. Make a ³/₄-inch cut in each corner of your kite, as shown in the above illustration. Fold and crease the edges of the paper between the cuts. The folded edges will form a hem for attaching the kite to the frame.

4. Make two marks on the center of your kite—one 15 inches down from

Tighten and string to bow

6 inches

X bridle points

2 inches

your top point and the second 2 inches from the bottom; these are your bridle points. Cut small holes in the kite at both points and reinforce the holes with tape on the back of the kite.

5. Turn your kite right side up and paint a picture of Berenice on it. You can add the stars of Coma Berenices, using the star map as a model. Use bright colors so that the stars stand out. (You can also paint another star map or a character from another legend on your kite.)

6. Once the paint is dry, lay the kite picture side down on a clean surface. Position the frame over the paper. Fold and glue the paper hem over the string on each of the four sides. Wait for the glue to dry.

7. Tie a string across the back of the cross-dowel by looping it through the notches. The string should pull the ends tight, making the cross-dowel bend slightly.

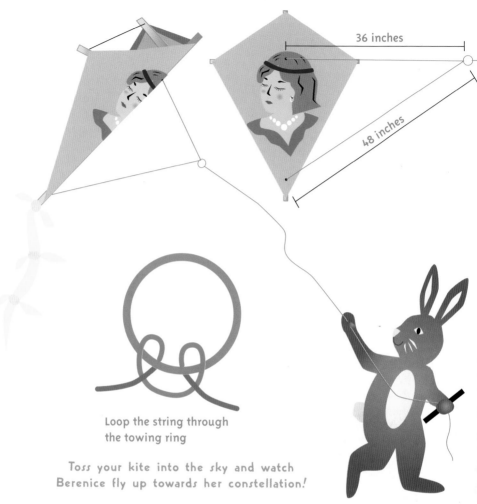

36 inches

48 inches

Loop the string through
the towing ring

Toss your kite into the sky and watch
Berenice fly up towards her constellation!

8. Loop a string 84 inches long through your towing ring. Tie a knot at the 36-inch mark. Pull the longer end of the string through the bottom bridle hole and tie it to the bottom end of the spine-dowel. Then, pull the shorter end of the string through the top bridle hole and tie it to the top end of the spine-dowel, as shown in the above illustration.

9. Tie your towing string to the towing ring.

10. You may want to add a tail to your kite. This can be made out of tissue paper or lightweight scraps of cloth and attached to the bottom of the spine-dowel.

# Cygnus
## The Swan

The ancient Greeks tell this story of Cygnus, the Swan. A boy named Cygnus (SIG-nus) had a good friend named Phaethon (FAY-uh-thun). Phaethon's mother Clymene (KLY-meen) lived on earth but his father was Helios (HEE-lee-os), the sun god. Phaethon wanted to prove to everyone that he was really the son of the god Helios. He set out to visit his father.

At the Golden Palace of the Sun, Phaethon was granted one wish by his father. Phaethon's wish was to drive the golden chariot that pulls the sun across the sky. Helios refused, fearing that his son would not be able to control the winged horses that led the chariot.

But Phaethon would not listen. He took off on the chariot the next morning without asking his father and ended up zigzagging across the sky, out of control. First he drove the chariot too low, causing fire damage on earth. Then he drove the chariot too high, angering constellations in the night sky, especially Leo (LEE-oh), the Big Bear, and Scorpio (SCORE-pee-oh). To save

the earth from burning up and to restore order to the heavens, Zeus threw a mighty thunderbolt at the chariot, blasting Phaethon right out of the sky. Zeus guided the sun back to its rightful place, and he turned Phaethon into a falling star. Phaethon crashed to Earth, falling to pieces in a raging river.

Cygnus, overcome with sadness at the loss of his friend Phaethon, dove into the dangerous river over and over again to retrieve all of the pieces of Phaethon. The friendship and courage Cygnus showed towards Phaethon touched both Helios and Zeus. To forever remind us of the importance of friendship, they placed Cygnus in the night sky as the diving swan, dipping his head into the water.

Our sun has so much energy that it can shine for 10 billion years.

# How to Find Cygnus

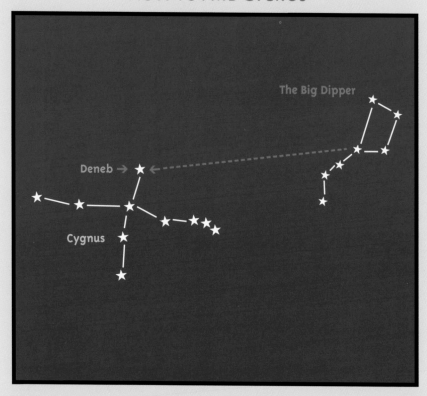

The best time of the year to find Cygnus is June through November. This swan's wings and neck are spread out, as if it is flying down towards the water. The brightest star in this constellation is called Deneb (DƐH-nehb). It is a very white star, and it marks the swan's tail. If you draw a line through the two stars of the Big Dipper's cup near the handle from the bottom up, and then across the sky, this will lead you to Deneb.

Cygnus is also called the Northern Cross.

# Constellation Theater-in-the-Round

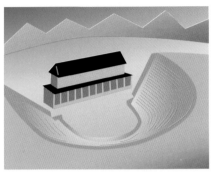

The ancient Greeks performed their plays outside. The audience sat in a semicircle around the stage. This was an early form of what we now call theater-in-the-round.

In Greek theater, the chorus helped guide the audience through the story of the play. The chorus's job was to comment on the play. The chorus stood to one side of the stage or below the stage, and the main actors took center stage.

Why not try acting out your own Greek play? Choose a director and actors. Make masks, costumes, and props for your play. You can put on an outdoor play about the story of Cygnus and have the audience sit in a circle around your stage. To reach the entire audience, project your voice and turn so all can see you.

## Paper-Bag Masks

### Materials
Paper grocery bags
Scissors
Tempera paint
Glue
Construction paper
Pens and pencils
Old magazines
Glitter
Cardboard

Cut space for shoulder

1. Fit your paper-bag mask by cutting spaces for your shoulders on the sides.

2. With the paper bag over your head, have a friend help you very lightly mark the spots in pencil where your eyes, nose and mouth are, making sure you do not poke your face.

3. Use a pencil to design a mask of your character, then cut out the holes for your eyes, nose and mouth. Use paint, pens, construction paper, magazine pictures, and glitter to decorate your mask. If you are Zeus or Helios, you are kings and you could use the glitter to make a crown. If you are Cygnus, you could paint a swan mask like the one pictured above. The chorus could wear the famous masks of theater—comedy and tragedy (one on front, one on back). See pictures of these masks on pages 54 and 55.

4. Put your character's mask on both sides of your bag so the audience sitting behind you can see your character's face too.

# Props and Costumes

Get creative and use stuff around the house for your props. For example, you can decorate a wagon or a bicycle to look like a chariot! Make your own props with anything you have permission to use and with the materials listed in *Paper-Bag Masks* on page 51.

| Props | Costumes |
|:---:|:---:|
| Sun | Sheets, scarves |
| Thunderbolt | Fun dress-up clothing |
| *(do not make corners too sharp)* | Belts |
| Golden chariot | Sandals |
| Golden Palace | Feathers |
| Wings for chariot horses & Pegasus | |
| Water | |
| Stars | |
| Broken pieces of stars | |

# The Play

The story of Cygnus has 6 main actors and a chorus:

Cygnus
Phaethon
Clymene
Helios
Pegasus
Zeus
Chorus
*(this can be one person or many people)*

## Scene 1

### Chorus

This is a story of the friendship between Phaethon and Cygnus, and how Cygnus became a constellation.

### Phaethon

My father is Helios, the sun god, who lives in the Golden Palace of the Sun.

### Chorus

We don't believe you.

### Phaethon

It is true, my father is a god.

### Chorus

We don't believe you.

### Cygnus

I believe you, Phaethon.

comedy

### Phaethon

Thank you, Cygnus, but it is not enough that you believe me. I will leave here and go to my father, and he will help me prove to these people that he is my father.

### Clymene
Don't go, my son. Stay here with me, your mother.

### Cygnus
Don't go, Phaethon. Stay here with me, your friend.

### Chorus
We don't believe you.

### Phaethon
I must go.

tragedy

## Scene 2
### Chorus
Phaethon arrives at the Golden Palace of the Sun.

### Phaethon
Father, I come from Earth where nobody believes that you are my father. Please help me prove that they are wrong.

### Helios
Phaethon, I will grant you one wish to help you.

### Phaethon
My wish is to drive the golden chariot that holds the sun across the morning sky.

### Helios
This wish is not a good one, my son. I fear that you will not be able to control the winged horses that lead the chariot. I cannot grant this wish. Come to me with another wish tomorrow.

## Scene 3
### (the next morning)
### Phaethon
Watch this! I WILL drive the chariot. WHOA!

## Chorus
## (the people on earth)

Put out the fire! Phaethon has lost control of the sun!

## Phaethon

I can't stop!

## Chorus
## (Leo, the Big Bear, and Scorpio)

Hey! Watch where you are going, Phaethon!

## Phaethon

I can't stop!

## Pegasus

Use this, Zeus! *(hands Zeus a thunderbolt)*

## Zeus

Ah, my trusty thunderbolt! Thank you, Pegasus—I'd better stop Phaethon and fast!

## Chorus

Ka-Boom!

## Scene 4

### Cygnus

Oh no! My friend, I told you not to go. I will gather every piece of you if it is the last thing I do.

### Zeus and Helios

Rise to the stars, young friend, and become the constellation Cygnus, the Swan. Whenever we gaze upon you, we will see you dipping into the water to gather your friend, and you will remind us of the importance of friendship.

### Chorus

The end.

56

**Stargazing**

**In the City and in the Country**

Have you ever noticed that when you are in the country it seems like there are a million more stars? Actually, it is just easier to see all the stars in the country because you are away from the competing lights of the city. It is also easier to see stars on a clear night when there are no clouds, rain, or fog to block your view.

Fill a knapsack with all the stuff on the Stargazing Equipment List. On a clear night, go to the country with your family or friends. Find a good spot to set up your telescope and start gazing! (If you don't have a telescope, binoculars or even a cardboard tube can help you focus better on individual constellations. But if you want to see all the constellations at once, nothing beats the naked eye!)

Use your star maps to find the constellations. Record in your notebook the date, time, location in the sky, and where you were when you first spotted the constellations. On another night do the same thing in the city. Notice any difference? Can you see more constellations in the country?

## Stargazing Equipment List

Telescope or binoculars or cardboard tube
Tissues (to clean telescope or binocular lenses)
Blanket (to spread out on grass)
Lawn chair
Notebook
Pens and pencils
Flashlight, red cellophane, rubber band
Star maps
Bug repellent

So you won't disturb your eyes' adjustment to the darkness, wrap the red cellophane around your flashlight with a rubber band, and use this while recording information in your notebook.

Here is a list of the constellations, asterisms, and stars included in this book. See how many you can find.

Ursa Major

Ursa Minor

The Big Dipper

The Little Dipper

Polaris (the North Star)

Merak

Dubhe

Leo

Regulus

Orion

Scorpio

Taurus

Canis Major

Canis Minor

Procyon

Sirius

Pegasus

The Great Square

Alpheratz

Coma Berenices

Cygnus

Deneb

# THE MILKY WAY GALAXY

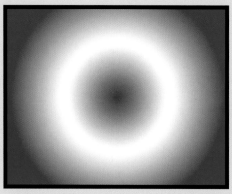 Shaped like a huge spiral, our galaxy is called the Milky Way. It is one of billions of other galaxies spread throughout the universe. Because Earth is located at the far end of the Milky Way, you can look out and see most of the Milky Way. Look for a wide band of white light in the sky. The best time to see the Milky Way in the Northern Hemisphere is from July through September.

Do you know why it is called the Milky Way? (Hint: it has nothing to do with a delicious candy bar!) The ancient Greeks gave it that name because it looks like spilled milk! Legend says that Hera spilled milk into the sky while feeding Zeus's infant son Hercules.

It is said that Phaethon (from the Cygnus story) followed the path of the Milky Way on his wild ride in the sun chariot. The Milky Way was also known as the path leading to the great castle of Zeus.

Our solar system includes Earth and all the other planets that revolve around our sun. It is positioned at the far edge of the Milky Way galaxy. Earth is positioned 30,000 light-years from the center of the Milky Way. The other planets in our solar system are Mercury, Venus, Mars, Jupiter, Saturn, Uranus, Neptune, and Pluto.

Light travels faster than anything else does, at 186,000 miles per second. One light-year is 6 million million miles, or the distance that light travels in one year. Astronomers use light-years to measure time and space. The Milky Way is 100,000 light-years across.